CAROLIN

BREAK THE CYCLES

DANGEROUS WARFARE PRAYERS AGAINST THE 14 WEAPONS OF THE ENEMY THAT CAUSES: DELAY, STAGNATION, CURSES, REJECTION AND SUFFERING.

BREAK THE CYCLES

DANGEROUS WARFARE PRAYERS AGAINST THE 14 WEAPONS OF THE ENEMY THAT CAUSES DELAY, STAGNATION, CURSES, REJECTION AND SUFFERING

BY

Caroline Wambugu

BREAK THE CYCLES

Copyright © By Caroline Wambugu

Tel: +254792703607

Email: cwambugu@gmail.com

Published by:

FLAP A WING PUBLISHERS (FAW PUBLISHERS)

+254792703607

Email: fawpublishers@gmail.com

Facebook: Flap A wing publishing house

www.fawpublishers.com

All rights reserved

No part of this publication may be reproduced, stored in a retrival system or transmitted in any form by any means, elecronic. mechanical, photocopying and recording or otherwise without the prior written permission of the Author.

Books authored By caroline Wambugu

BOOKS ON PERSONAL GROWTH & DEVELOPMENT

1) Am I a Prophet? Know the four-fold faces of a prophet and understand the prophetic ministry.

2) Shadows of Triumph: A mystery of humble beginnings, success and pain.

3) Spiritual combat: Mastering the Art of warfare in the spiritual realm.

4) The power of transformation: No one is too small to make a difference.

5) Rise from the Ashes: Navigating the spiritual wilderness

6) I am known by a different Name

7) Break the Cycles: Warfare prayers against the 14 weapons of the enemy.

8) Flap a wing Journal: Learn how to soar

9) Success is a gift

CONTENTS

INTRODUCTION..8

THE WEAPON OF ARROWS/ SWORDS........................... 10

HORNS OF DARKNESS..15

MAGIC CHARMS/VEILS/NETS.................................... 19

HOUSEHOLD ENEMIES... 22

DESTINY HIJACKERS & EXCHANGERS......................28

SPIRITUAL GATES...32

WITCHCRAFT...42

SPIRITUAL SLUMBER..46

SATANIC CONSPIRACY..53

HIGH PLACES & EVIL SACRIFICES...........................56

WRONG IDENTITY & NAME.....................................59

FILTHY GARMENTS..62

EVIL YOKES & BURDENS..65

SPIRITUAL BLINDNESS...68

INTRODUCTION

For years I faced severe difficulties and spiritual warfare. I tried to find personal testimonies of people who were facing any form of spiritual warfare. I found some but I desired more. I begun to write my own experiences not knowing that one day they would become a series of books.

Initially, I would talk to everyone about the forces I was fighting but most of them thought I was crazy or they would look at me strangely wondering what I was talking about. Finally, I decided to talk to a few trusted people who gave me advice and others offered encouragement.

You are where I was and I am here to tell you that you are not alone. You are battling powers, forces and evil spirits and wondering what is going on? You seem to be fighting forces that few seem to understand. God has not abandoned you. God takes a vessel through strange, deep and terrible processing, standing at nothing and touching everything so that *the vessel becomes the message.* The message is brought about by actual experiences.

In this book, I highlight *some of the weapons I encountered in spiritual warfare, what is their effect and prayers against them.*

Who Should Read Break the Cycles

- *Those seeking to know the nature and strategies of the Enemy.*
- *Those who have been hidden and have been contending for a longtime in spiritual warfare.*
- *Those individuals who have been waiting for the manifestation of a God-given dream or Vision.*
- *Those individuals whom God has called and feel they have been hidden in the womb of the spirit.*
- *Individuals seeking to understand the strategies and devices of the enemy.*
- *Adults seeking to understand what is holding them back from their true potential.*
- *For Faith Based Organisations to reveal the importance and the role of spiritual weapons to their members.*
- *For Change Agents who want to arise and impact their generations.*
- *For Kingdom business men and women who want to have dominion in the marketplace.*
- *For educators who can use it for one on one training, in groups and in structured programs.*

Caroline Wambugu
Founder of Faw publishers,
An Author, a Transformational speaker and a Minister of God.

THE WEAPON OF ARROWS/SWORDS...

EPHESIANS 6:16 says in every battle you will need faith as your shield to stop the fiery arrows(darts) aimed at you by Satan.

WHY DO WE NEED TO PRAY AGAINST ARROWS/SWORDS?

These are **invisible attacks** against us- spiritual arrows are invisible attacks from the kingdom of darkness targeting a person, a group of persons, or a family.

These arrows cause injury, and death (premature death of people, ministry, relationships, businesses, finances), They are also arrows of affliction (sicknesses, rejection, losses, oppression, weariness, stagnation, discouragement), and Arrows of division and confusion.

These invisible attacks/arrows are manifested as words.

One night I had trouble sleeping. I was tossing on my bed and at the same time I felt a lot of grief and my spirit was troubled. I knew something was wrong but I didn't know what it was. After tossing for a long time I asked the holy spirit, "Lord, what is wrong?".

He didn't reply. Because sometimes the Holy Spirit speaks to me in open visions and dreams.

I drifted to sleep expecting a response.

A few minutes later the Lord opened my eyes, and I was a woman in a room and this woman was doing incantations. My photo and other photos of believers were mounted on the wall and she was enchanting against us. The holy spirit drew my attention to the speakers.

I realized what this woman was saying was being amplified in the spiritual realm and disturbing my spirit. Even though in the physical it was quiet in the spiritual realm my spirit was being troubled by those spiritual speakers and evil words.

What am I saying? The enemy is wicked and he can use words to attack you, your family, or your territory. That is why you can find in a territory there is a particular spirit troubling people; immorality, confusion, backwardness, drunkardness, etc.

God has given us his word to rule and enforce authority in our lives, family, and territory. It is your responsibility to nullify words spoken to steal, kill, and destroy your life.

RELATED SCRIPTURES

PSALMS 59;6 They come at night snarling like vicious dogs as they prowl the streets. Listen to the filth that comes from their mouths, the piercing swords that fly from their lips." Who can hurt us? They sneer'.

PSLMS 57:4 My soul is among lions; I lie among the sons of men who are set on fire. Whose teeth are spears and arrows. And their tongue a sharp sword."

PSALMS 91:5 You shall not be afraid of the terrors of the night nor the arrow that flies by day

PRAYERS POINTS (IN ITALIC BOLD)

 # We ask God to increase our faith- Believing faith, Speaking, and doing faith because the shield of faith quenches the arrows of the enemy.

"I CORINTHIANS 3:6 Paul planted, Apollos watered and God gave the increase. To many Christians faith is confidence, trust, assurance, trust or belief and this is true according to the bible but there I more to faith than these words convey.

2 CORINTHIANS 4:13 Yet we have the same spirit of faith as he who wrote, I believed and therefore have I spoken. We too believed and we spoke.

PSALMS 116:10 Psalmist said," I believed therefore I spoke.

We can see faith involves elements of believing and speaking. Faith is in our spirit.

 # We ask the holy spirit to give us the spirit and gift of faith

The Holy Spirit is the source of all gifts. A spiritual gift is given to the whole church as a means of helping the entire church.

1 CORINTHIANS 12:7 The Spirit gives to one faith, words of wisdom, words of knowledge, Gifts of healing, working of miracles, prophecy, Discerning of spirits, Diverse tongues, and interpretation of tongues.

So there is the gift of faith and spirit of faith.

We come against every flying arrow released against us."
"PSALMS 91:5 You shall not be afraid of the terrors of the night nor the arrow that flies by day.

We ask God to break the arm or the hand that throws them."
"PSALMS 10:5 Break the arm of the wicked and the evil man. Seek out his wickedness until you find none."

EZEKIEL 30:22 Therefore thus says the Lord God, "Surely I am against Pharaoh king of Egypt, and I will break his arms, both the strong one and the broken one and I will make the sword fall out of his hand.

We rise against every tongue releasing judgement over my life.
"ISAIAH 54:17 No weapon formed against shall prosper, And Every tongue which rises against you in judgment you shall condemn."

We are releasing the arrows of the lord against our enemies to completely destroy and conquer them." "2 KINGS 13:17 Then he commanded, open that eastern window, and he opened it. Then he said," Shoot!" so he did. Then Elisha proclaimed," This is the lord's arrow, full of victory over Aram, for you will completely conquer the Arameans at Aphek. Now pick up the other arrows and hit the ground."

We are releasing the sword of the spirit which is the revealed word of God. 2 CORITHIANS 10:4 Our weapons of warfare are mighty in God.

HEBREWS 4:12 For the word of God is living and powerful and sharper than any two-edged sword, piercing even to the division of soul and spirit, and of the joints and marrow, and a discerner of the thoughts and intents of the heart.

2

HORNS OF DARKNESS...

ZECHARIAH 1:18 *I lifted my eyes and I beheld four horns.... these horns come to scatter and ensure no man will lift his head.*

A horn is a symbol of power, an altar, a person.

Horns **can represent a person** as seen in REVELATIONS 5:6....and in the midst of the elders stood a lamb as though it had been slain, having seven horns and seven eyes, which are the seven spirits of God sent out into all the earth.

Horns **can represent an altar** as seen in EXODUS 27:2 God told moses to make a bronze altar. This altar had four corners or horns and sat in the courtyard.

Horns **can represent powers** as seen in ZECHARIAH 1:18 I lifted my eyes and I beheld four horns…. these horns come to scatter and ensure no man will lift his head.

In DANIEL 7 **we see the horns have eyes to see and a mouth to speak evil.** There was a horn that had human eyes and a mouth that was speaking blasphemous words/arrogantly and this horn was waging war against the saints of God and was prevailing over them.

In Daniel 7:25 we have assurance God will make a judgment in our favor and **take away the horns kingdom, power, and authority.**" He shall speak pompous word against the most high, Shall persecute the saints of the most high God And shall intend to change times and law. Then the saints shall be given into his hand for a time and times and half a time. But the court shall be seated and they shall take away his dominion. To consume and destroy it forever and it shall be given to the saints."

WHY DO WE NEED TO PRAY AGAINST THE HORNS OF DARKNESS?

Horns come to scatter our destinies, finances, marriages, children, destiny helpers, and everything in our lives. As I said horns can represent a person, a power, an altar, or a covenant. Some people in our lives are **horns the enemy is using to fight us** or it may be an altar. God tells Gideon you are mighty and you are going to serve me but before you do this you need to deal with an evil altar raised in your father's house- Gideon defiles the altar. There are altars raised as horns in our families that are fighting us and we cannot serve God effectively until they are dealt with.

Horns come to fight our worship, prayer, believers, and ministries according to Zechariah 1:19b (NKJV)...These are the horns that have scattered Judah(worship), Israel (God's elect), and Jerusalem(ministry/church). The horns raised against us fight against our praise and worship (Judah means praise), the horns fight the chosen people of God, you and I (Israel means God's chosen people), and the horns fight Jerusalem, (this is church or ministries.)

Horns ensure no man could lift up his head as seen in v21 of Zechariah..." So no one could lift up his head." When we talk about head this means authority, power, control, sight, and confidence. That is why in some families' people always work for others, some are poor or you find everyone relying on one person to help the entire family, or people are born in servitude, etc.

PRAYER

"We come against every northern horn, southern, eastern, western horn raised against the purposes of God in our lives/church/ and we declare that the purposes of God over our lives will be accomplished."

"We rise against every tongue that releases words of judgment over our lives."

God to cut off the horns of the wicked and exalt the horn of our power, influence, impact, holiness, wisdom, finances, business, marriage, and anointing. "

"PSALMS 75:10 All the horns of the wicked I will also cut off. But the horns of the righteous I will exalt."

PSALM 92:10 But my horn you have exalted like the horn of a unicorn/wild ox; I have been anointed with fresh oil.

Lord, annoint me with fresh oil for battle
God according to DANIEL 7:25 Make a judgement in our favour and take away the horns kingdom, power and authority and give it to the saints.

4

MAGIC CHARMS/VEILS/NETS...

Ezekiel 13:18 Prophesy against them and say, thus says the lord," Woe to the women who sew magic charms on their sleeves and make veils for the heads of people of every height to hunt souls! Will you hunt the souls of my people and keep yourselves alive?

VS 20 Therefore thus says the Lord God; Behold I am against your magic charms by which you hunt souls there like birds. I will tear them from your arms and let the souls go the souls you hunt like birds.

VS 21 I will also tear off your veils and deliver my people out of your hand and they shall no longer be as prey in your hand. Then you shall know that I am the lord.

WHY SHOULD WE PRAY AGAINST MAGIC CHARMS, VEILS OR NETS?

In our times the enemy uses charms like; magic rings, bracelets, and other jewelry **to attack believers and to steal from them.** Also, these pieces of jewelry **can enslave the souls of people/ blind people,** especially in churches where the so-called "self-proclaimed prophets" wear them and call them healing bracelets.

The wearer of magic charms **causes the souls of people to fly.** Many people wake up and feel tired and worn out because at night their souls were summoned and witchcraft performed on them.

When veils are cast over a person/territory this can result in **spiritual blindness or a heavy layer of darkness preventing people from praying.** Also, when a veil is cast over a person it **can hinder their glory and this person will be overlooked, poor, ignored, and humiliated at every turn.**

Nets can ensnare the souls and blessings of people. The enemy stations nets along the roads to catch the souls of people and their blessings.

Also, nets can be like the cobwebs a spider makes and the enemy uses this **to entrap the prayers of believers.**

PRAYERS

#*"God tear the magic charms on their sleeves they use to hunt for souls like birds and let those souls go"*

#*"God to tear their veils and deliver his people out of their hand and God's people shall no longer be their prey."*

#*"We ask God to frustrate their signs and drive these diviners mad"*

ISAIAH 44;25 Who frustrates the signs of the babblers, And drives diviners mad: Who turns wise men backward and makes their knowledge foolishness.

#*"Destroy the nets of the wicked that capture victims and blessings, destroy them by fire in Jesus' name."*

PSALMS 10:9(NLT) Like lions they crouch silently, waiting to pounce on the helpless. Like hunters, they capture their victims and drag them away in nets…. V16 The helpless are overwhelmed and collapse; they fall beneath the strength of the wicked.

#*"God to send for many fishers to fish them out and many hunters to hunt them from every mountain and every hill and out of the holes of the rocks.*

JEREMIAH 16:16 Behold I will send for many fishermen," says the Lord, and they shall fish them; and afterward, I will send for many hunters, and they shall hunt them from every mountain and every hill, and out of the holes of the rocks.

HOUSEHOLD ENEMIES...

MATTHEW 10:36 Your enemies will be right in your household.
MATTHEW 12:25.... A city or home divided against itself is doomed.

There are our relatives, brothers, sisters, grandmothers, fathers, uncles, aunts, and even friends who have alliances or covenants with powers of darkness and wicked spirits in the heavenly realm to oppress people's lives, steal, kill, and destroy.

The household enemies will use spirits to fight you

WHY PRAY AGAINST HOUSEHOLD ENEMIES?

Block your access to resources, destiny helpers

They destroy your harvest

They will curse you

Release a spirit of war to fight everything in your life.

Release bondage and yokes in your life

Release an enslaving spirit

Release oppression, depression, and discouragement in your life
Cause you to change focus from God to worldly pleasures
Release Lukewarmness and compromise in your life

Block your access to resources, destiny helpers

NUMBERS 20:20 The spirit of Edom blocks access and makes something intended to be short very long, something intended to be very easy becomes very hard, to multiply your sweat, to frustrate you, and cause you to give up prematurely.

PP(prayer); JOB 19:8 Every fenced path that stops me from moving forward be broken in Jesus' name.

They destroy your harvest

They use the spirit of the Midianites to destroy your harvest. They will allow you to labor and then come and destroy your harvest.

JUDGES 6:3 So it was, whenever Israel had sown, the Midianites would come up; also Amalekites and the people of the east would come up against them, then they would encamp against them and destroy the produce of the earth…leaving them with no sustenance. So Israel was impoverished because of them.

Ask God to restore what the enemy has killed, stolen, and destroyed.

JOEL 2:25 So I will restore to you the years….

Ask God to build a hedge around us, our household, and everything that belongs to us.

JOB 1:10 Have you not made a hedge around him, around his household, and around all that he has on every side?

They will curse you

The Spirit of Balaam is a territorial spirit fueled by envy. When it sees you have made notable progress it will do all it can to curse you and pull you down. It raises 21 altars to come against you and offers blood sacrifice.

Prayers-NUMBERS 23:23 For there is no sorcery against Jacob, Nor any divination against Israel. It now must be said of Jacob and of Israel," Oh, What God has done!"

ISAIAH 54:15 All who gather against me shall fall for my sake....

Release a spirit of war to fight everything in your life.

Release the spirit of the philistine to fight everything in and around your life; fight your peace, joy, finances, relationships, children, husband, and wife.

God lifts up a standard against what the enemy is doing in my life; Increase my peace and finances, safeguard my relationships, my children, my health, my business

ISAIAH 59:19 So they shall fear the name of the lord from the west, and his glory from the rising of the sun; When the enemy comes in like a flood, the spirit of the lord will lift up a standard against him.

Lord keep everything in my life and around my life in perfect peace

ISAIAH 26:3 You will keep him in perfect peace, whose mind is stayed on you because he trusts in you.

Release bondage and yokes in your life

Pharaoh's spirit is the spirit that puts you under bondage and yokes.

Prayers; Every yoke be broken in my life, finances, business, and every bondage destroyed.

ISAIAH 54:17 No weapon formed against you shall prosper and every tongue that raises in judgement I shall condemn.

Release an enslaving spirit

This is the spirit of Egypt that causes you to labor

I am breaking off every form of slavery (rebellion, habit, effortless labor, religion, sin) that has tied me and I ask God to pull me into his kingdom.

ROMANS 6:17 But God be thanked that though you were slaves of sin, yet you obeyed from the heart that form of doctrine, to which you were delivered. (obeyed the new teaching which God has given you). And having been set free of sin you became slaves of righteousness.

They terrorize and release fear in your life

This is the spirit of Assyria that puts fear in you.

God you have good plans for my life, you will strengthen me and uphold me in your righteous right hand. "JEREMIAH 29:11-14 For I know the plans I have for you," says the lord. They are plans for good and not for disaster, to give you a future and a hope. In those days when you pray. I will listen.

Lord, end my captivity and restore my fortunes. Lord, gather me out of where you sent me and bring me back to my inheritance.

If you look for me in earnest, you will find me when you seek me. I will be found by you," says the lord. I will end your captivity and restore your fortunes.

I will gather you out of the nations where I sent you and bring you home again to your own land."

Lord, stregthen me and uphold me with your righteous right hand.

"ISAIAH 41:10 Fear not, for I am with you. Be not be discouraged, for I am your God. I will strengthen you. Yes, I will help you. I will uphold you with my righteous right hand."

#Release oppression, depression, and discouragement in your life

They release the spirit of the Canaanites that sits on believers to cause them to begin to sin or go back to doing what God had delivered them from.

Prayer; *I will be far from oppression, fear, and terror.*

ISAIAH 54:14 In righteousness you shall be established; You shall be far from oppression, for you shall not fear. And terror, for it shall not come near you and indeed they shall surely assemble but not because of me. Whoever assembles against you shall fall for your sake.

#Cause you to change focus from God to worldly pleasures

They release the spirit of the perizzite to cause you to abandon the call of God and go back and begin to do other activities.

PRAYER

I will be established in righteousness.

ISAIAH 54:14 In righteousness you shall be established; You shall be far from oppression, for you shall not fear. And terror, for it shall not come near you and indeed they shall surely assemble but not because of me. Whoever assembles against you shall fall for your sake.

God to pour upon me a spirit and grace for prayers and supplication....

ZECHARIAL 12:10 I will pour upon you a spirit and grace for prayers and supplications…

I will give myself continually to prayer and read and meditate on the word of God.

ACTS 6:7 We will give ourselves continually to prayer and the ministry of the word.

God give me the hunger for your word.

#Release Lukewarmness and compromise in your life

You lack seriousness in prayer, church, and fasting and you begin to compromise.

PRAYER

Lord, create in me a hunger for your word and thirst for right living.

MATTHEW 5:8 Blessed are those who hunger and thirst for righteousness for they shall be filled.

PRAYER

God circumcise my heart so I can love you with all my heart, soul, body, and mind. God turn my heart towards you as you would a river.

"DEUTRONOMY 30;6 And the lord your God will circumcise your heart and the hearts of your descendants, to love the lord your God with all your heart and with all your soul, that you may live."

PROVERBS 21:8 The king's heart is in the hand of the lord, like the rivers of water; He turns it wherever he wishes.

6

DESTINY HIJACKERS & EXCHANGERS...

In Matthew 2:1-2 We see how diviners/astrologers from the east said to Herod when Christ was born," We have seen his star as it arose and we have come.....

These men were following the star of Christ and when you read the commentary of this scripture it reveals they had seen the star 2 years before Jesus was born. In the Kingdom of Darkness, some forces study stars and pursue them to steal, kill, and destroy.

WHY PRAY AGAINST DESTINY HIJACKERS/ EXCHANGERS?

Because your star represents your glory. The brighter your star the more glorious we have. That is why we have football stars, Hollywood stars, academic stars, etc.

Stars represent destinies and if your star is stolen, manipulated, exchanged, or caged by powers of darkness it will be hard to know and fulfill your destiny. You will be like a shadow; insignificant, mediocre, harsh life, etc.

Star carries your glory. The word glory means; radiant, light and it symbolizes greatness, honor, fame, excellence, magnificence, eminence, wealth, riches, power, and recognition.

If anyone steals your star/glory they have stolen your honor (lack of honor brings shame and disgrace), and you will be poor, live as a servant, and be insignificant.

That is why ECCLESIASTES 10:17 says, "I have seen servants upon horses and princes walking as servants upon the earth.

This means an exchange of stars/destiny the problem is not that the princes are walking, it is that they are walking as servants, living as servants.

There are so many people whose glory has been stripped away from them according to JOB 19:9 He hath stripped me of my glory, and taken the crown from my head. When this happened to Job he lost everything, he became an object of ridicule, accusation, and mockery and lived in poverty.

HOSEA 9:11 Says, "As for Ephraim, their glory shall fly away like a bird, from the birth and from the womb and from the conception.

We see here how words have the power to cause a whole tribe to lose their glory. As seen in this scripture your glory can be stripped from you, and your family in conception, in the womb, and after birth.

Is there hope for you? Yes, there is hope because God promises us in his word that he is a restorer.

PRAYING FOR THE GLORY OF GOD TO BEGIN MANIFESTING IN THE CHURCH, OUR LIVES, FAMILY & BUSINESS,

We renounce lives that are not ours. Today we are demanding repossession of what belongs to us.

Release wholeness in every area of your life in spirit, heart, body, marriage, and finances.

PSLAMS 90:16-17 Let your work appear to your servants and your glory to their children. V17 and let the beauty of the lord our God be upon us, And establish the work of our hands for us. Yes, establish the work of our hands.

#Let your glory, Oh God begin to manifest in us so that sorcery and divination has no power over us.

NUMBERS 23:23 For there is no sorcery against Jacob, nor divination against Israel,,,,It now must be said of Jacob and of Israel: Oh, what God has done.(Witchcraft will not work because God must be glorified in us).

#let your glory, Oh God begin to manifest in us to give us influence with all men and mighty men in this land and far-off lands.

MARK 1:36-37…they followed after him and said all men seek for thee.

GENESIS 37:9….The sun, the moon, and eleven stars bowed down to me.

ZECHARIAH 8:23 "This is what the lord almighty says; In those days ten people from nations, and languages around the world will clutch at the hem of one's Jews robe. And they will say," Please let us walk with you. For we have heard that God is with you.

#Let your glory. Oh God begin to manifest in us so we can receive aid from rulers, wealth from powerful kings and mighty nations.

PSALMS 45:12 The princes of tyre will shower you with gifts. People of great wealth will entreat your favor.

ISAIAH 60:10/14/16 Foreigners will come to rebuild my cities. Kings and rulers will send me aid……. v14b those who despised you will come and kiss my feet……V16 Powerful kings and mighty nations will bring the best of their goods to satisfy your every need. You will know at last that I the lord am your savior and redeemer.

6

SPIRITUAL GATES...

UNDERSTANDING AND DEALING WITH SPIRITUAL GATES

A gate is an entry or an exit point.

There are 2 types of gates: physical gates and spiritual gates.

Every physical gate has a corresponding spiritual gate. We need to understand before we can conquer the spiritual gate first.

Upon every gate there are strongmen, the gate can be opened for you, but the strongmen prevent you from entering therefore we need to know HOW TO COMBAT the strongmen at the gate and have them defeated.

1 CORINTHIANS 16:9 For a great and effective door has opened to me, and there are many adversaries.

Spiritual gates are places of **POWER AND CONTROL** and whoever possesses the gates controls the territory. Godly altars in a place open a gate of entry for God in that place while evil altars open the gate for Satan to enter and control that environment and infiltrate the lives of people in that environment.

Experiences of people having dreams of masquerades or ghosts or snakes chasing them or having sex, swimming, and eating are an indication of satanic altars made possible by spiritual gates or gates of hell providing points of entry.

Satanic gates become a **STUMBLING BLOCK** to a person's spiritual growth and progress in different areas of their lives. Such gates can prevent a person from getting married of if they prevent them from getting babies, they can also prevent them from experiencing financial breakthroughs, education, and growth in the ministry.

Some churches planted in certain areas come under the yoke of principalities, ruling that territory, and hardly experience growth until they PRAY and UNSEAT the territorial demons sitting on the spiritual gates of that territory. This happened to Paul as he went to preach the gospel in Athens and Ephesus.

In ACTS 17:16-34 Paul resisted in Athens because there were evil spiritual gates situated there.

In Acts 19:23-41 Paul was resisted in Ephesus because there were evil spiritual gates situated there.

The Bible says the gates of hell should not prevail against us, even if we find ourselves in a territory controlled by evil spiritual gates.

MATTHEW 16:19

We should not be ignorant lest Satan take advantage.

2 CORINTHIANS 2:11 Lest Satan take advantage of us; for we are not ignorant of his devices.

The Bible says we must **POSSESS THE GATES OF OUR ENEMIES** IN GENESIS 22:17..In blessing I will bless you, in multiplying I will multiply your descendants as the stars of heaven and as the sand which is on the sea-shore; and your descendants shall possess the gate of their enemies.

Also, GENESIS 24:60 Says they blessed Rebekah and said to her: "Our sister, may you become the mother of thousands of ten thousand; And may your descendants possess the gates of those who hate them.

Gates are strengthened by the presence of gate men that is why witches and wizards go around barefoot in the early hours of the morning, strengthening their evil gates using the law of the word of God in DEUTRONOMY 11:24 "Every place on which the sole of your foot treads shall be yours; from the wilderness and Lebanon, from the river, the Euphrates, even to the western sea shall be your territory.

These witches/wizards bring the people and resources in that city under their control.

As believers in Christ every time we are entering the gates of the city, we should command evil gates in that city to lift up their heads and let the king of glory come in.

PSALMS 24:7 Lift up your heads, O you gates! And be lifted up, you everlasting doors! And the king of Glory shall come in.

We should RAISE AN ALTAR FOR God through prayer and fasting and we should call upon the name of the Lord because he is always desiring to help us open the gates that are shut against our lives, our families, and the church.

ISAIAH 45:2 I will go before you and make the crooked places straight; I will break in pieces the gates of bronze and cut the bars of iron.

We need to command the desolations to lift away and we destroy the gates of hell over that area in Jesus name.

PRAISE AND WORSHIP are 2 keys of heaven that God has given us to open satanic gates.

MATTHEW 16:19

HOW DO WE POSSESS OUR GATES?

1) YOUR STAR MUST BE INTACT

Your star pulls into your life the things or events that your destiny needs to be fulfilled. Witches and wizards use people's stars for their own benefit and when that happens the victims find it difficult to manifest their destiny and good things hardly come their way.

MATTHEW 2:9 When they heard the king, they departed and behold, the star which they had seen in the East went before them, till it came and stood over where the young child was.

When a child is born, its star appears spiritually in heaven and can be accessed by the wicked forces and they can tamper with it.

Prayer: We pray to God for revelation concerning our star and ask him to restore back our star if it has been tampered with by wicked forces.

2)OUR DESTINY MUST BE INTACT

Destiny is the book written about you by God by which you are sent on earth to execute.

PSALMS 40:7 Then said I, Lo, I come; in the volume of the book it is written of me.

LUKE 4:17 Jesus opened the scroll written about him," The scroll containing the message of Isaiah was handed to him, and he unrolled the scroll to the place where it says;

V18/19 This is what is written of me, who I am, why I am here, and what I am meant to accomplish.

In JOHN 1:21 The Jewish leaders wanted to know who John is and John tells them in V23 John replied in the words of Isaiah;" I am a voice shouting in the wilderness, prepare a straight pathway for the Lord's coming!".

3)WE MUST RAISE ALTARS FOR GOD EVERYWHERE WE GO LIKE ABRAHAM

We raise altars by living a righteous life, an obedient life, and a life of sacrifice and commitment unto God, and also raise them by declaring the word of God that will overthrow any satanic altar in every place.

1 SAMUEL 5:2-6

POSSESSING THE GATES OF YOUR ENEMIES

1)For you to possess the gates of your enemies YOU MUST BE A FRIEND OF GOD; Walk in obedience to God.

ROMANS 8:14

Genesis 22:17

JOHN 15:14-15

2) You must have some LEVEL OF COMMITMENT to the kingdom of God and there must be some exploits.

LUKE 10:17, 10:19 The disciples committed themselves to preaching the word of God.

3) You must be ANOINTED WITH POWER by the holy spirit.

ACTS 10:38

PRAYERS

ISAIAH 28:5-6, 29:6

We thank God for revelation on spiritual gates then we receive anointing to deal with all the gates prevailing against us, our family, and our church.

We receive the SPIRIT OF JUSTICE to sit in judgment against the satanic devices against us.

We receive strength to flush the enemy out of our gates in the name of Jesus Christ.

We release thunder, earthquakes, great noise with storms, and tempest with devouring fire to totally destroy every satanic gate restricting our progress in Jesus's name.

HOSEA 7:12, MATTHEW 18:18, AMOS 7:4

Rebuke Satan out of my life/church/family in the name of Jesus Christ.

By the holy spirit's power arrest, all the spiritual gatemen working against us, family, and church bind them and cast them down into the pit of fire in Jesus's name.

PROVERBS 14:19, PSALMS 147:13

Thank God for his covenant that evil shall bow before the good and the wicked shall bow at the gates of righteousness.

Demand the disarming of every evil spirit and wicked person at my gate. Let every evil spirit be judged at my gates. We shut the gates permanently against the wicked in the name of Jesus.

Command every stealing and affliction by the wicked in my life/family/church to stop in Jesus's name

ISAIAH 45:1-3

Thank God for taking my right hand to subdue nations and lose the armor of kings.

Open the two leaved gates so that they will remain open as my blessings keep flowing in.

Ask God to make every crooked places be straight and to break the gates of bronze and bars of iron before me in Jesus' name.

Ask for real treasures of darkness and hidden riches of secret places to be given to you/family/church.

I thank you, God, I declare you are my father and king.

OTHER PRAYERS CONCERNING GATES

1 CORINTHIANS 16:9 For a great and effective door has opened to me (for a great work), and there are many adversaries.

There is always warfare at the gates.

WHY DO WE NEED TO PRAY FOR OPEN GATES/ OPEN DOORS?

Adversaries don't just follow men but doors. Between one season to another is a door. There are seasons of transition e.g. a door from the living room to the the dining room. If the door is closed you will remain in that season for a long time.

Because there are spirits assigned against our gates/doors to prevent us from going through to access our inheritance, blessings

Because the enemy makes wicked decisions upon the gates that affect our destinies.

Also, there are doors we need the Lord to close; Doors allowing entrance of evil spirits in our lives and doors allowing misfortune to fight us or addictions and evil habits.

I had no job for a long time and I began to fast and pray to get a breakthrough. Then one night the Lord appeared and gave me a message. I saw the television opposite me turn on and these words flashed on the screen; -

Opening doors

Opening doors

Opening doors

Then a voice said," Please, be patient Caroline."

I received a well-paying Job abroad after a while.

What am I saying? There are some requests we have asked of the Lord but there seems to be no answer nor any change, this is because there are doors that God needs to open for you.

PRAYERS

 # Lord, open for me my doors according to REVELATION 3:7 And to the Angel in the Church of Philadelphia write," These things says he who is holy, he who is true," he has the key of David, he who opens and no one shuts, and shuts and no one opens."

 # "Pray against every adversary of my open doors/gates e.g. Doors of ministry, influence, finance, marriage, family"

1 CORINTHIANS 16:9 For a great and effective door has opened to me (for a great work), and there are many adversaries.

 # "Every spirit assigned by the devil to stand against the corridors connecting one season and another of my life. I come against and I engage the power in the blood of Jesus and the power in the word.

#ISAIAH 45:2 The word states The lord has gone before to level the mountains, He has gone before to smash the gates of

bronze and cut through bars of iron to give me the treasures hidden in the darkness-secret riches so that I may know he is God.

#PSALMS 24:7 The word also states ancient gates and ancient doors, must lift up their head so the king of Glory who carries my inheritance may come in.

Satan used 3 gates to lock Peter.

Acts 12:10 When they were past the first and the second guard posts, they came to the iron gate that leads to the city, which opened to them by its own accord, and they went out,,,,,

"The 3 gate/iron gate that leads to the city to open on its own accord in Jesus' name. This gate that leads to the city is the gate of visibility, and influence. If this gate does not open the city will not acknowledge you."

"We come against every wicked decision that was made or has been made upon the gates to steal, kill, and destroy our lives, to oppress and afflict".

The Destiny of Ruth was decided upon the gates by Boaz, a relative of Naomi and ten elders of the city

RUTH 4;1 Now Boaz went up to the gate and sat down there… …a relative of Naomi and ten men elders of the city…."

#*We call forth our destiny gatekeepers and men of influence to go up to our Godly ordained gates to secure our destinies by speaking in our favor, releasing the resources we need to advance our destiny, secure our godly inheritance, and release our blessings.*

We are untying our colt tied by the door outside on the street. That colt was needed to fulfill prophecy and destiny.

MARK 11:4 So they went way, and found the colt tied by the door outside on the street/crossroads and they loosed it.

Every destiny helper sent by God, but is tied we lose you now in Jesus' name.

7

WITCHCRAFT....

Witchcraft is the use of alleged supernatural powers of magic. A witch is a practitioner of witchcraft. Traditionally, "witchcraft" means the use of magic or supernatural powers to inflict harm or misfortune on others.

WITCHCRAFT INVOLVES THIS PROHIBITED PRACTICES

Laws prohibiting various forms of witchcraft and divination can be found in the books of Exodus, Leviticus and Deuteronomy. These include the following (as translated in the Revised JPS, 2023 :

Exodus 22:18 – You shall not tolerate a sorceress.

Leviticus 19:26 – You shall not eat anything with its blood. You shall **not practice divination or soothsaying.**

Leviticus 20:27 – A man or a woman **who has a ghost or a familiar spirit** shall be put to death; they shall be pelted with stones—and the bloodguilt is theirs.

Deuteronomy 18:10-11 – Let no one be found among you who **consigns a son or daughter to the fire,** or **who is an augur, a soothsayer, a diviner, a sorcerer, one who casts spells, or one who consults ghosts or familiar spirits, or one who inquires of the dead.**

COMMON SIGNS YOU'RE UNDER WITCHCRAFT ATTACK

\# You keep dreaming of being attacked by snakes.

\# You hear your name being called and there's no one there. Sometimes voices tell you to kill yourself.

\# Sicknesses that keep shifting in the body and cannot get proper and definite diagnosis

\# Anyone who tries to help you suddenly gets an issue that eats up the help they were to give you.

\# Sources of finances suddeny dry up for you and your destiny helpers.

\# Relationship and Marriage Conflicts: If you consistently experience conflicts and problems in your relationships, especially when you believe you have found the right person, it could be a sign of a witchcraft attack.

\# Money and Financial Problems: Persistent financial difficulties, despite your hard work and efforts, can be a sign of being under a spell or curse. If money seems to constantly elude you and you struggle to make ends meet, it may be worth considering the possibility of a witchcraft attack.

BREAK THE CYCLE

\# Unexplainable Sickness: If you experience unexplained health issues that doctors cannot diagnose or treat effectively, it could be a sign of witchcraft or a curse. This is particularly true if you feel your health deteriorating despite medical interventions

\# Promise and Fail: If people consistently make promises to help you but fail to follow through, it may indicate the presence of a curse or spell. This can manifest in various areas of life, such as job opportunities or assistance from others.

PRAYERS

 # Heavenly Father I ask you to forgive me of the sins I committed against you or anybody made in your image.

In the name of Jesus and by His Spilled Blood on the cross I rebuke all witchcraft attacks in Jesus name against me and my children. I bind every wicked work, every alter risen against me and my children. I strike it into pieces by the rod of Yahshua Jesus Christ. I call Holy Spirit fire to burn it into ashes in Jesus name. I set ablaze every blood sacrifice against me and my children by Holy Spirit fire in Jesus name.

 # I bind block and break every familiar spirit trying to come against me and my children our lives in Jesus name. I put every familiar spirit in chains and fetters dipped in the blood of Jesus. I muzzle them with the blood of Jesus so they shall not speak against us in Jesus name. I tossed them into the lake of fire to leave us alone in Jesus name.

 # In the name of Jesus, I bind and break witchcraft, witchcraft control, mind-binding spirits, spirits that block and/or bind the will, mind control, destruction, lust, fantasy lust, perversion, intimidation, rebellion, rejection, schizophrenia, paranoia, anger, hatred, wrath and

rage, resentment, bitterness, unforgiveness, slander, unteachableness, deception, doubt, unbelief, passivity, pride and false humility.

 # God visit every witch in my life, land, my family with your judgment.

 # Everything that represents witchcraft activity in and around my life is destroyed in the mighty name of Jesus.

 # Every prediction and divination made by witches against my life, my family, finances, business, and health be destroyed in Jesus' name.

 # Declare 2 PETER 1:3 as his divine power has given to us all things that pertain to life and godliness through the knowledge of him who called us by glory and virtue.

 # Declare COLOSSIANS 3:2 For you died, and your life is hidden with Christ in God.

Prayer is a weapon God has given you.

Prayer is an armor God has given you.

Prayer is all conquering, invisible weapon of the army of God.

 # Please Holy Spirit bless us with your peace love and healing in Jesus name we pray. Bless us with your presence protection wisdom knowledge and favor guidance through the Holy Spirit in Jesus name amen.

SPIRITUAL SLUMBER...

JUDGES 16:19 Then she lulled him to sleep on her knees, and called for a man and had him shave off the seven locks of his head. Then she began to torment him and his strength left him.

DANGERS OF SPIRITUAL SLEEP
1) THE ENEMY WILL SHAVE OFF YOUR SEVEN LOCKS AND TAKE AWAY YOUR VISION

JUDGES 16:19 Then she lulled him to sleep on her knees, and called for a man and had him shave off the seven locks of his head. Then she began to torment him and his strength left him.
The Lord will depart from you.
V20 and she said," The Philistines are upon you, Samson" so he awoke from his sleep, and said, I will go out as before, at other times, and shake myself free!". But he did not know the lord had departed from him.

The enemy will take out your vision and you become a captive

V21 Then the Philistines took him and put out his eyes, and brought him down to Gaza. They bound him with bronze fetters, and he became a grinder in the prison.

PRAYERS

 # God deliver me from the lap and lull of Delilah. Reveal every spirit of Delilah released against my life.

Give me discernment to discern it and shake myself free of it.

 # Lord, I desire to abide in your presence, reveal and remove every hindrance set by the enemy to drive me away from your presence.

 # Lord, restore my vision and set me free from every spiritual, mental, and physical captivity.

 # Lord, let my hair begin to grow again-my hair of prayer, strength, word, hunger for your word and my glory

V22 However the hair on his head began to grow again after it had been shaved.

 # Lord, give me strength to take vegeance on my enemies.

V28...O Lord God, remember me, I pray! Strengthen me, I pray, just this once, O, God, that I may with one blow take vengeance on the Philistines for my two eyes!".

 # Let the spirit of the Lord begin to move upon me again.

JUDGES 13:25 And the spirit of the lord began to move upon him at Mahaneh dan between Zorah and Eshtaol.

2)YOUR ENEMY WILL PREVAIL AND REJOICE OVER YOUR DEFEAT

PSALMS 13:3 Consider and hear me, O lord my God: Enlighten

my eyes, lest I sleep the sleep of death; V4 Lest my enemy say, "I have prevailed against him, "Lest those who trouble me rejoice when I am moved.

 # Lord, consider and hear me enlighten my eyes so my enemies will not prevail nor rejoice over my defeat.

3) YOU CAN NOT DISCERN DANGER

JONAH 1:4 But the Lord sent out a great wind on the sea, and there was a mighty tempest on the sea so that the ship was about to be broken up. V5 Then the mariners were afraid; and every man cried out to his god, and threw the cargo that was in the ship into the sea, to lighten the load. But Jonah had gone down into the lowest parts of the ship, had lain down, and was fast asleep.

4) WHEN YOU SLEEP THERE ARE VISIONS YOU CAN NOT SEE, NOR HEAR

ZECHARIAH 4:1-2 Now the Angel who talked with me came back and wakened me, as a man who is wakened out of his sleep. V2 And he said to me, "What do you see?".

5) SPIRITUAL SLEEP WILL CAUSE YOU TO ENTER INTO TEMPTATIONS

MATTHEW 26:40 Then he came to the disciples and found them sleeping, and said to Peter," What! Could you not watch with me one hour? v41 watch and pray, lest you enter into temptation, The spirit indeed is willing, but the flesh is weak.,v43 And he came and found them asleep again, for their eyes were heavy.

6) SPIRITUAL SLEEP VEILS GOD'S GLORY

LUKE 9:32 But peter and those with him were heavy with sleep;

and when they were fully awake, they saw his glory and the two men who stood with him.

CURE FOR SPIRITUAL SLEEP

1)New life from the holy spirit

JOHN 3:3 Jesus replied," I assure you, unless you are born again, you can never see the kingdom of God.

V4 What do you mean, "Am I to enter my mother's womb and be born again?"

V5 Jesus replied," The truth is none can enter the kingdom of God without be born of water and spirit. v6 Humans can only reproduce human life, but the holy spirit gives new life from heaven.

2)Be watchful and strengthen the things that remain and are ready to die

REVELATION 3:1-2 And to the angel of the church in Sardis write," These things says he who has the seven spirits of God and the seven stars; I know your works, that you have a name that you are alive, but you are dead. V2 Be watchful, and strengthen the things which remain, that are ready to die, for I have not found your works perfect before God.

Strengthen your prayer life, study and meditate on the word of God, and your relationship with God.

LUKE 18: Jesus spoke a parable to them, that men always ought to pray and not lose heart.

DEUTRONOMY 17:18-20 Also it shall be, when he sits on the throne of his kingdom, that he shall write for himself a copy of this law in a book, from the one before the priests, the Levites.

V19 It shall be with him, and he shall read it all the days of his life,(WHY?) that he may learn to fear the lord his God and be careful to observe all the words of this law and these statutes V20 that his heart may not be lifted above his brethren, that he may not turn aside from the commandment to the right or to the left, and that he may prolong his days in his kingdom, he and his children in the midst of Israel

WHAT DISCIPLINES DO I NEED TO HAVE

1)Time to pray by yourself

MATTHEW 14:23 And when he had sent the multitudes away, He went up on the mountain by himself to pray. Now when evening came, He was alone there.

2)There are some problems you face that require two weapons; prayer and fasting

MATTHEW 17:21 However, this kind does not go out except by prayer and fasting.

3)Time to go into the temple

ACTS 3:1 Peter and John went to the temple one afternoon to take part in the three o'clock prayer service.

4)Time to Join with other believers

ACTS 2:42 They joined with other believers and devoted themselves to the apostle's teaching and fellowship, sharing in the lord's supper and prayer.

Fellowship; a feeling of friendship between people who do things together or share an interest, aim, or belief.

5)Invest time to grow in the word of God

JOHN 6:63 It is the spirit who gives eternal life. Human effort accomplishes nothing. And the very words I have spoken to you are spirit and life.

The word of God is spirit and carries life.

CONCLUSION

WHEN YOU SLEEP SOMETHING CAN BE PLANTED

MATTHEW 13:25 But that night as everyone slept, his enemy came and planted weeds among the wheat.

.... his enemy came and planted......when you are in a spiritual sleep there are things the enemy plants....

ASK EZEKIEL 8:8...God tells Ezekiel to dig into the wall, he did and uncovered a hidden room. V10 So I went in and saw the walls engraved with all kinds of snakes, lizards, and hideous creatures and also saw the various idols worshipped by the people of Israel.

WHEN YOU SLEEP SOMETHING CAN BE TAKEN AWAY

GENESIS 2:21 And the Lord God caused a deep sleep to fall on Adam, and he slept; and he took one of his ribs, and closed up the flesh in its place.

BREAK THE CYCLE

 # My God, You are a merciful God. Awaken me, Oh Lord, from this spiritual slumber and set my feet upon the Rock. Make me a watchman and a light bearer that is always alert and prayerful. Help me to put on the armor of light in the mighty name of Jesus Christ.

Ephesians 6:18 Praying always with all prayer and supplication in the Spirit, being watchful to this end with all perseverance and supplication for all the saints.

Romans 13:11 And do this, understanding the present time: The hour has already come for you to wake up from your slumber, because our salvation is nearer now than when we first believed.

 # I pray that you would give me the grace and the strength to overcome any spiritual slumber and to embrace your will for my life.

"But those who hope in the Lord will renew their strength. They will soar on wings like eagles; they will run and not grow weary, they will walk and not be faint." – Isaiah 40:31

"Awake, O sleeper, rise up from the dead, and Christ will give you light." – Ephesians 5:14

9

SATANIC CONSPIRACY...

WHAT IS A CONSPIRACY?

A combination of men for an evil purpose; an agreement between two or more persons, to commit to steal, kill and destroy.

More than forty had made this conspiracy in Acts 23:13.

ACTS 23:12 The next morning a group of Jews got together and bound themselves with an oath to neither eat nor drink until they had killed Paul.... went to the leading priests and other leaders and told them what they had done. They involved them in a conspiracy. Influenced them to use their power and authority to have Paul brought to them...we will kill him on the way. V16 but Paul's nephew heard of the plan and went to the fortress to tell Paul.

PRAYERS

 # I nullify every demonic and Satanic conspiracy over my life, business, finances, and family.

 # I terminate, neutralize, and destroy the oaths, covenants, and evil sacrifices they have bound themselves with.

 # Lord, deliver me from every strategy of my enemies, their plans, plots, traps, and snares.

Warfare involves tactics and strategies. The greatest generals are great tacticians and strategists. You cannot win without a strategy. Don't allow the enemy to strategize against you. Overcome and destroy his strategies through prayer. Traps and snares are hidden. People fall into traps unknowingly. We are delivered from the snare of the fowler.

A fowler is a hunter. Satan is the hunter of souls. We can release ourselves and others through prayer. The main tactic of the enemy is deception. He is a liar and the father of lies. The Word of God exposes the tactics of the enemy. God is light, and His Word is light. The light exposes the enemy and tears away the darkness.

 # Let their counsel fail, turn their counsel into foolishness or to nothing, let them fall for my sake, the sake of your work.

ISAIAH 7:5-7 Because Syria, Ephraim, and the son of Remaliah have **taken evil counsel against you** saying, v6 Let us go against Judah and trouble it, and let us make a gap in its wall for ourselves, and set a king over them, the son of Tabeel' V7 Thus says the Lord GOD: "It shall not stand, Nor shall it come to pass."

ISAIAH 8:10 Take counsel together, but it will come to nothing; Speak the word, but it will not stand. For God is with us.

 # Lord, let every strategy from hell be exposed and brought to light.

 # Lord, let your plans, and purposes for my life prevail. The plans to bless me, prosper me, satisfy me with a long life, and plans for peace and good health.

10

HIGH PLACES & EVIL SACRIFICES...

What are high places?

High places, very simply, **were places of worship on elevated pieces of ground.** High places were originally dedicated to idol worship (Numbers 33:52; Leviticus 26:30), especially among the Moabites (Isaiah 16:12). These shrines often included an altar and a sacred object such as a stone pillar or wooden pole in various shapes identified with the object of worship (animals, constellations, goddesses, and fertility deities). It seems that, at times, high places were set up in a spot that had been artificially elevated; 2 Kings 16:4 seems to differentiate the "high places" from the "hills."

The Israelites, forever turning away from God, practiced Molech worship and built high places for Baal (Jeremiah 32:35). Although Solomon built the temple of God in Jerusalem, he later established idolatrous high places for his foreign wives outside of Jerusalem and worshiped with them, causing him the loss of the kingdom (1 Kings 11:11). The people were still sacrificing at the pagan high places before the temple was built, and Solomon joined them. After the Lord appeared to him in a dream at Gibeon, the king returned to Jerusalem and sacrificed offerings; however, he continued to waver between the two places of worship.

Not all high places were dedicated to idol worship. They played a major role in Israelite worship, and the earliest biblical mention of a site of worship, later called a "high place," is found in Genesis 12:6–8 where Abram built altars to the Lord at Shechem and Hebron. Abraham built an altar in the region of Moriah and was willing to sacrifice his son there (Genesis 22:1–2). This site is traditionally believed to be the same high place where the temple of Jerusalem was built. Jacob set up a stone pillar to the Lord at Bethel (Genesis 28:18–19), and Moses met God on Mt. Sinai (Exodus 19:1–3).

Joshua set up stone pillars after crossing the Jordan (Joshua 4:20) and considered this a high place of worship because the Israelites "came up from" the Jordan onto higher ground. The high places were visited regularly by the prophet Samuel (1 Samuel 7:16). High places as sites of Canaanite idol worship Judges 3:19) extended into the period of Elijah (1 Kings 18:16–40). God would name only one high place where sacrifice was authorized, and that was the temple in Jerusalem (2 Chronicles 3:1). God commanded that all other high places be destroyed. King Josiah destroyed them in 2 Kings 22—23.Priests, people operating in the high places and when they come they release decrees over people, family, businesses.

SCRIPTURE ON HIGH PLACES

JEREMIAH 48:35 Moreover, says the lord, I will cause to cease in Moab the one who offers sacrifices in the high places and burns incense to his God.

PRAYERS

Lord, arise and cause to cease in my family, city one who offers sacrifices in the high places and burns incense to their gods.

Lord, I arise to pull down, overthrow, and destroy every wicked altar established in the high places.

Lord, destroy every strange god and altar in the high places. Destroy every high place erected by my forefathers from generations past. 2 KINGS 18:4

Lord, quench every fiery fire being burnt in the high places.

Lord, destroy every wicked word, spell, incantation, oath, and wicked power and wicked words released on those wicked high places.

Lord, let the high places be made desolate, altars laid to waste and made desolate, your idols may be broken and made to cease, your incense altars may be cut down and your works may be abolished. EZEKIEL 6:6

Lord, let not the high places be rebuilt again 2 CHRONICLES 33:3

Lord, set me on my high places (PSALMS 18:33)

Lord, cause me to ride in the high places eat produce of the fields, draw honey from the rock, and oil from the flinty rock.

WRONG IDENTITY & NAME...

MARK 10:46...Blind Bartimaeus, son of Timeous sat by the road begging.
He was called blind Bartimaeus.

WHY PRAY AGAINST THE WRONG IDENTITY/NAME?

So many of us are carrying the wrong names in the spiritual realm. So our names correlate to the circumstances that we are going through. You may be called a reject, a loner, poor, timid, or shy based on how people see you.

Similarly, many times, a person's name holds special meaning. Children today might be named after family members to show respect or to honor their memory. After marriage, a woman usually changes her last name to signify the beginning of the next chapter. But what we fail to realize is that some of these names may be attached to evil covenants, evil dedications, or misfortunes.

We see Jabez in the bible given a name that brought pain to his life.

That is why we see God changing the name of Abraham, Jacob, and even Peter.

When Rebekah's pregnancy was full of trouble. When She cried out to God why she was suffering God told her what she carried were not babies but nations.

However, the children struggled in Rebekah's womb. She said, "If it is thus, why is this happening to me?" (Gen. 25:22, ESV) and went to the Lord in prayer. And the Lord said to her:

"Two nations are in your womb, and two peoples from within you shall be divided; the one shall be stronger than the other, the older shall serve the younger." —Gen. 25:23

When Jacob was born his name limited him in every way until God came and changed it to Israel, the nation of Israel. What am I saying? There are people amongst us who carry a name not meant for them; a name of limitation while they are meant to carry and birth nations.

PRAYERS

 # Lord, I terminate, nullify, and come against every wrong identity I carry in the spiritual realm that I go by in the physical. Any wrong identity that has been bestowed by wicked forces, people, challenges, or circumstances. Wrong identity of shame and scorn.

 # Lord, I come against every wrong identity that has caused me to sit by the road begging, not to arise.

 # Lord, restore my true name and identity.

 # Lord, establish me and make my name great, lord give me a name in Kenya and nations.

 # Lord, give me a name of honor and recognition.

This is Elisha, who served Elijah-mighty man. Recognized the men were with Jesus. Let my name to a name associated or connected to power, wealth, and influence.

 # Lord, I receive a new name which your mouth will name.

PSALMS 112:2a His descendants will be mighty on earth.

 # Lord, I arise and throw aside every evil garment that has been bestowed by evil forces to give me the wrong identity of begging, shame, reproach, lack, oppression, reproach, and ridicule.

 # Lord, clothe me with rich robes and desire to follow you.

FILTHY GARMENTS...

ZECHARIAH 3:1-6 Then he showed me Joshua the high priest standing before the angel of the lord, and Satan standing at his right hand to oppose him. And the Lord said to Satan," The Lord rebuke you, Satan! The Lord who has chosen Jerusalem rebuke you! Is this not a stick snatched from the fire?

Now Joshua was clothed with filthy garments and was standing before the Angel. Then he answered and spoke to those who stood before him, saying," Take away the filthy garments from him." And to him, he said, "See, I have removed your iniquity from you, and I will clothe you with rich robes."

PRAYERS

Pray against every spirit assigned by the devil against us to oppose us on every side, encamp around us when the seed is sown, and destroy it. (The spirit of the Midianite, Amalekite, and spirit from the east)

 # Prayers God to remove the filthy garments from us

God remove every filthy garment on my body, life, business, church

Destroy every evil garment of sickness, lack, rejection, poverty, shame, affliction, spells, negative words, accusations, shame, sickness, witchcraft, failure, and humiliation over my life, business, finances, family, and church. Let the evil garments catch fire in the name of Jesus.

 # Ask God to remove iniquity from us and clothe us in rich and perfumed robes.

….See, I have removed your iniquity from you, and I will clothe you with rich robes."

ISAIAH 61:3 God has clothed me with the garments of praise.

GENESIS 37:3 Put on me the garment of favor like Joseph.

ISAIAH 61:10 I will greatly rejoice in the lord. My soul shall be joyful in my God; For he has clothed me with the garments of salvation, He has covered me with the robe of righteousness….

PSALMS 45:8 Your robes are perfumed with myrrh, aloes, and cassia….

Besides being used on people, the Bible tells us anointing oil was also used in making clothing fragrant.(Myrrh kingship/worship/preservation,aloes(Healing/preservation),cassia(greek word for cinnamon it represent passion/fire

 # Lord, clothe me in rich robes annointed with myrrh so I can offer pure worship unto you.

 # Lord, clothe me with rich robes annointed with aloes so I can release healing whereever I go; spiritual healing, emotional healing, financial healing, family healing, marriage healing within me and

around my life.

 # Lord, clothe me with rich robes annointed with cassia to ignite my life with fire/passion for prayer, worship and holliness.

Let me also be a channel to ignite the fire of your word and prayer in the souls of men.

JUDGES 6:3 So it was, whenever Israel had sown, the Midianites would come up; also Amalekites and the people of the east would come up against them, then they would encamp against them and destroy the produce of the earth…leaving them with no sustenance. So Israel was impoverished because of them.

PP: Ask God to restore what the enemy has killed, stolen, and destroyed.

JOEL 2:25 So I will restore to you the years….

 # Ask God to build a hedge around us, our household, and everything that belongs to us

JOB 1:10 Have you not made a hedge around him, around his household, and around all that he has on every side?

God has released grace to accomplish and breakthrough we will engage the power in the word.

JOB 22:28 Whatever you decide to do will be accomplished and light will shine on the road ahead of you.

EVIL YOKES & BURDENS...

ISAIAH 10:27 It shall come to pass in that day that his burden will be taken away from your shoulder, and his yoke from my neck, And the yoke will be destroyed because of the anointing

WHY WE SHOULD PRAY AGAINST YOKES?

A Satanic **instrument of oppression** used to limit a person's growth, promotion, and fulfillment. Breakthrough, etc. It is a hindering barrier.

A Satanic **device that sponsors affliction** in the lives of people. 1st Kings 12:11 And now whereas my father did lade you with a heavy yoke, I will add to your yoke: my father hath chastised you with whips, but I will chastise you with scorpions. Friends, you cannot negotiate with Satan. The dark places of this earth are full of the habitation of cruelty. EVERY power assigned to prolong your problems, may the ground open up and swallow them in the MIGHTY name of Jesus!

A yoke is something **that places the destiny** of a man in the hands of the enemy. A prisoner cannot eat what he pleases or go anywhere he wants to. In Acts 12:6 we are told that Peter was in prison between two soldiers bound with TWO chains and there were keepers who kept the prison door!!! The only thing that could free the destiny of Peter was a divine intervention. You will be released TONIGHT!!!

Deuteronomy 15:1 At the end of every seven years thou shalt make a release.

The Bible tells us in Deuteronomy 15:1 that at the end of every seven years, thou shall make a release.

THE MANIFESTATIONS OF THE YOKE/BURDEN

1. Sin:

When a man cannot work with God or is easily attached to a particular thing that stands against the will of God.

2. The Yoke of Sickness:

Not every sickness is normal. Some are caused by external forces. The woman of the issue of blood spent 12 years in this yoke.

3. Demonic Patterns:

A particular display of evil forces. It can come with barrenness, failures, setbacks, near-success syndrome, and delays (marriage, promotion, achievement), when these things happen around you, just know that you are under a yoke

C] Mysteries of Yoke

1. Your speed, movement, and direction is determined by the Yoke around your neck

2. Yoke brings about limitations. There is a certain level you can't cross.

3. It brings sorrow, pain, death, etc.

4. If you don't deal with the yoke, it will keep dealing with you. It doesn't go by crying, or negotiations. Yokes can only give way by order through genuine encounter with the Lord.

PRAYERS

 # Let every burden my enemies, witches, household enemies, wicked spirits have placed on my shoulders, life be removed.

 # I removed his shoulder from the burden; His hands were freed from the baskets (PSALMS 81:6)

 # Let, every burden be removed from my life physical, spiritual, witchcraft burden, financial burden, business burden, and family burden be removed from my life. Every burden of my enemies is removed from my life.

 # Let, every yoke be removed from my neck. The yoke of limitation, the yoke of lack and poverty, the yoke of sickness

 # Every yoke is destroyed by the power, the anointing of the holy spirit.

 # Holy Ghost, command my release from failure, poverty, stagnancy, profitless hard labor, etc. by fire.

Isaiah 9:4-5 For thou hast broken the yoke of his burden, and the staff of his shoulder, the rod of his oppressor, as in the day of Midian. For every battle of the warrior is with confused noise, and garments rolled in blood, but this shall be with burning and fuel of fire.

14

SPIRITUAL BLINDNESS...

2 KINGS 6:18-20 *And when they came down to him, Elisha prayed unto the lord and said," Smite this people, I pray thee, with blindness. And he smote them with blindness according to the word of Elisha.*

And Elisha said unto them, this is not the way, neither is this the city; follow me, and I will bring you to the man whom you seek. But he led them to Samaria. And it came to pass, when they were come into Samaria, that Elisha said, "Lord, open the eyes of these men, that they may see. And the lord opened their eyes, and they saw; Behold, they were in the midst of Samaria.

Elisha prayed and said...smite these people with blindness. And he smote them according to the word of Elisha.

To smite means to strike with a firm blow or to strike with a heavy blow with a weapon or the hand.

To smite means to attack or afflict suddenly and harmfully.

PRAYER 1

2 KINGS 6:18-20 And when they came down to him, Elisha prayed unto the lord and said," Smite this people, I pray thee, with blindness. And he smote them with blindness according to the word of Elisha.

 # Lord, deliver my spiritual eyes and vision from undue influence by the kingdom and forces of darkness.

 # Lord, every word released, and every weapon deployed by dark forces to hinder my spiritual vision be destroyed in the name of Jesus.

 # Lord, your word says you are the shade at my right hand and the sun shall not strike me during the day nor the moon at night. # Lord, I break and rebuke every evil deity and force operating through the sun, moon, and stars to afflict my spiritual eyes, hindering my vision in the name of Jesus.

JUDGES 5:20 They fought from the heavens; The stars from their courses fought against Sisera.

PRAYER 2

And Elisha said unto them, this is not the way, neither is this the city; follow me, and I will bring you to the man whom you seek. But he led them to Samaria.

 # Lord, deliver me from every evil power station on the way to my destiny, on my path that is assigned to misdirect my steps.

PSALMS 59:3 For look, they lie in wait for my life(soul); The mighty gather against me, Not for my transgressions nor my sin, O, lord.

JOHN 21:18b…but when you are old, you will stretch out your hands, and another will gird you and carry you where you do not wish.

Lord, deliver me from every voice of the enemy camouflaged as the voice of the holy spirit.

JOHN 16:13 However, when he the spirit of truth, has come, He will guide you into all truth; for he will not speak on his authority but whatever he hears he will speak; and he will tell you things to come.

Lord, guide me into all truth to be able to distinguish enemies camouflaged as helpers.

Lord, position the right people beside and around my life so I can walk and actualize my destiny.

Lord, open my eyes to see the real faces of my enemies and discern the intents of hearts.

PRAYER 3

And Elisha said unto them, this is not the way, neither is this the city; follow me, and I will bring you to the man whom you seek. But he led them to Samaria.

Lord, deliver me from every Samaria my enemies have led me to.

ISAIAH 30:21 Your ears shall hear a word behind you, saying, "This is the way, walk in it, "Whenever you turn to the right hand or whenever you turn to the left. (NKJV).

ISAIAH 30:21 Whether you turn to the right or the left, your ear will hear a voice behind you, saying," This is the way to walk in it.

Lord, give me a hearing ear and a seeing eye.

Holy Spirit guide me at all times, in all things, and cause me to be tuned to your divine signals and directions at all times.

Lord, I rebuke every spiritual deafness in the name of Jesus.

Let every evil power having a grip on my vision and dreams be broken in Jesus' name.

Lord, make my spiritual visions clear and plain in Jesus' name.

PRAYER 4

DANIEL 2:22 "He revealeth the deep and secret things; he knoweth what(is)in the darkness, and the light dwelleth with him.

Lord, your word says "He revealeth the deep and secret things; he knoweth what(is)in the darkness, and the light dwelleth with him.

Lord, reveal the deep and secret things concerning my life, destiny, assignment, purpose, my family.

Lord, you know what is in the darkness....Lord, reveal what is in the darkness/hidden fighting my life, breakthrough, finances.

Lord, be my light and let this light dawn on me,

JOHN 8:12 When Jesus spoke again to the people, he said, I am the light of the world. Whoever follows me will never walk in darkness, but will have the light of life.

REFERENCES

https://www.rccgvictorytemple.org/biz-just-released/

https://breadoflifevoice.com/understanding-evil-yokes-their-nature-types-negative-influences-ex-51-21/

https://www.gotquestions.org/high-places.html

https://www.prayerrequest.com/threads/prayers-against-witchcraft-attacks-and-familiar-spirits.4839573/

Other books by Caroline Wambugu

Spiritual combat: Mastering the Art of Warfare in the Spirit Realm

In this book, I highlight actual experiences of some of the spiritual warfare I have gone through, the dimensions of truth that saved me and as a demonstration of the power of God.

Who Should Read mastering the art of spiritual warfare in the spirit real?
- *Those who have been hidden and have been contending for a longtime in spiritual warfare.*
- *Those individuals who have been waiting for the manifestation of a God-given dream or Vision.*
- *Those individuals whom God has called and feel they have been hidden in the womb of the spirit.*
- *Individuals seeking to understand the strategies and nature of spiritual warfare.*

Rise from the ashes: Navigating the spiritual wilderness

Your suffering is a precursor of the greatness and abundance about to be manifested in your life. When the darkness ends, the wilderness ends, and the veil is flipped you will be blinded by the glory about to be revealed.

In this book you will learn:
- √ How adversity plays an important role in your spiritual growth and maturity.
- √ How to navigate through the wilderness experience.
- √ Understand that spiritual wilderness is a phase you will have to go through regardless of who you are.
- √ Understand the butterfly system; how it forms and its colour symbolism in your life.
- √ Understand the butterfly effect and your importance in shaping destinies.
- √ Understand how spiritual abortion occurs.
- √ Access devotional content to help you through adversity.

The power of transformation: No one is too small to make a difference. In this book I inspires the reader to take action, I emphasize that every individual regardless of age or status, has the power to make a difference. With unwavering determination this book serves as a rallying cry for men and women to arise and change the trajectory of their lives, their families, their marriages, their churches and their nations.

Who Should Read No One Is Too Small To Make A Difference?

- *Those who have been hidden and have been contending for a longtime in a spiritual wilderness.*
- *Those individuals who have been waiting for the manifestation of a God-given dream or Vision.*
- *Those individuals who God has called and feel they have been hidden in the womb of the spirit.*
- *Individuals or youth activists seeking to inspire and change their families, schools and their generation.*

BREAK THE CYCLE

Made in the USA
Coppell, TX
28 April 2025